P9-CRP-500

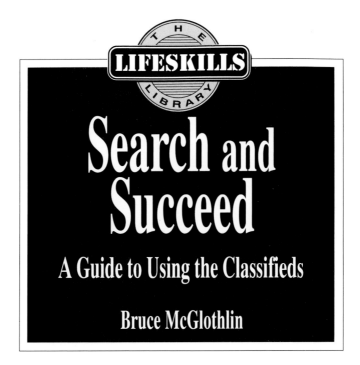

# LIFESKILLS LIBRARY

# Search and Succeed

## A Guide to Using the Classifieds

### Bruce McGlothlin

# THE ROSEN PUBLISHING GROUP, INC.
# NEW YORK

Published in 1994 by The Rosen Publishing Group, Inc.
29 East 21st Street, New York, NY 10010

First Edition
Copyright 1994 by The Rosen Publishing Group, Inc.

Manufactured in the United States of America.

**Library of Congress Cataloging-in-Publication Data**
McGlothlin, Bruce.
    Search and succeed: a guide to using the classifieds / Bruce McGlothlin
       p.    cm. — (The lifeskills library)
    Includes bibliographical references and index.
    ISBN 0-8239-1695-2
    1. Advertising, Classified—Juvenile literature. [1. Advertising,
Classified.]. I. Title. II. Series. III. Series: Life skills library.
HF6126.M34  1994
659.13'2—dc20
                                                  93-47545
                                                  CIP
                                                   AC

# CONTENTS

# INTRODUCTION

**S**ince turning sixteen several months ago, Nicholas has wanted two things—a part-time job and a used motorbike. He feels that having these things will mark his entrance into the adult world. Unfortunately, his search has been very disappointing.

Nicholas has been going door-to-door in town, looking for a part-time job. He has discovered that most businesses are not hiring part-time workers. Others are hiring only full-time workers who are older and more experienced.

He has also checked with the school guidance office to see if they know of any jobs. The counselor said that this year no employers had contacted the school to look for part-time workers.

---

The classified section of the newspaper offers information about job opportunities and items for sale.

Nicholas's search for a used motorbike has proved just as frustrating. He has asked friends who own motorcycles if they know of anyone who might be selling one. He has even posted a sign at the local motorcycle shop. No one has responded.

After these disappointments, Nicholas is very uncertain about how to look for a part-time job, and about how to buy a used motorbike. He is beginning to feel very low.

A few days later, Nicholas is talking about his frustrations to some of his friends. One of them asks if he has checked the classified ads. Nicholas answers yes, rather than admit to not knowing what classified ads are. His friend mentions they are found in the local newspaper. Since Nicholas does not particularly like to read, he has never even considered the newspaper as a possible source of information. But now he is curious. What are the classified ads? Where are they in the paper? How do you read them? How do you make contacts? These are only some of the questions Nicholas is thinking as he goes to buy a newspaper.

## Maria's Problem

For a long time, Maria has wanted to buy a car. She has always dreamt that owning a car would give her more freedom.

Her parents had told her if she would raise the money for the car, they would help her with the insurance payments.

One day Maria discovered that a neighbor was offering for sale a used blue convertible with low mileage. It was in good shape mechanically, and the price was $300, which made it a pretty reasonable deal. Maria was excited about the idea of working to pay for it. So she got a part-time job and began saving money.

Maria was slowly making progress toward her goal when her neighbor informed her he needed the money right away. He said he would like to hold the car for her, but someone else had made an offer of cash which she could pay by the end of the month.

If Maria could not raise the cash in a week or so, she would lose the car. Maria needed $300 in a week's time. What could she do?

Maria told her parents about this, hoping they would give her the money, but they continued to say that she must raise the money herself. She respected their decision because she had assumed the responsibility for buying the car.

Discussing her situation with friends led to several ideas. A few friends offered to lend her the money from their savings, but she did not like that idea. Other friends thought her parents should just give her the $300. That was out of the question.

Then one of her friends suggested she have a garage sale. Of course! Why didn't she think of that before?

Her parents had been after Maria to clean out the garage for some time now. There were many things in it that were in good condition and could be sold for cash.

When Maria told her parents about the idea, they thought it was a terrific one. However, there was a great deal of work to do in a short period of time.

Garage sales are a good way to make money, but people need to hear about them. "Garage hunters" scan the newspapers daily for garage sales. Maria must use the classified ads to inform people about the time and place of her sale. But she has never placed an ad before. How should Maria go about this? How much does it cost? Where should she start?

Let's talk about the classified ads as a valuable source of information for young people such as Nicholas and Maria.

# WHAT ARE CLASSIFIED ADS?

**P**eople are always on the lookout for things they want. This could be jobs, apartments, keyboards, cars, pets or other things they need. They may also have things they want to sell. But how do people find out about buying and selling these types of things?

They may be like Nicholas or Maria—who need to learn more about one of the most popular and easy methods of buying and selling—the classified ads.

The word "class" means a group of people, things, or qualities, having common characteristics.

The classified ads organize and arrange groups of things, under descriptive headings, called classes. This is why the ads are called "classified."

Classifying things under headings like HELP
WANTED, makes things easier to find.  It saves
time and provides a quick reference.

"Ad" is a short word for advertisement.  Ads are
public notices, or announcements about buying and
selling.  They can refer to goods or services.  The
goal is to make a deal with someone.

Some great bargains can be found by searching
classified ads. Another name for the classifieds is the
want ads.  They spread the word about goods and
services to many people.

## Sources

One good source for classified ads is the daily newspaper, especially one that also publishes on Sunday.
Although some ads may run every day, the largest
number of ads usually appear on Sunday.  Because
most people have more time to read the paper on
that day, the chances of reaching more people are
much better then.  So advertisers spend more
money for Sunday ads.  This is the reason that
Sunday papers are often large and bulky.  They
are loaded with retail and classified advertising.
Retail ads are store ads.

In general, the classified section is the most popular and widely read section of the newspaper.  It
provides a good source for information that is
updated every day.

—

**Some ads encourage you to call for more information.**

Another valuable place to find classified ads is in the back of specialty magazines or trade publications. These are usually read by people who have specific interests.

These magazines may appear only once a month. They are usually distributed over a wide geographic area and their ads reach people whose interests are similar to those of the advertisers. However, making a deal could involve communication and travel expenses. But to people buying or selling specialty items this may not be a problem when they find something that they really want.

Other sources include local advertising magazines or "green sheets," as they are often called. These offer goods and services within a specific local area. Most are published weekly and are distributed free. Large numbers of people often read these carefully because they are always in search of bargains. They enjoy the idea of shopping to save money.

## Newspaper Classifieds

As a rule, newspapers offer the longest and best organized lists of classified ads. These ads are presented in an easy-to-read and easy-to-use format so that people can find the goods and services they are searching for.

All newspaper classifieds are listed in the Classified Section. Look for the exact page in the index.

—

**Classified ads can lead consumers to some great bargains.**

The Classified Section is subdivided under general categories, where all goods and services are placed.

Most newspapers list general categories such as:

1. Special Interests
2. Employment
3. Rentals
4. Real Estate
5. Financial
6. Home Improvement
7. Merchandise
8. Pets
9. Farms and Lawns
10. Hobbies
11. Outdoor Sports
12. Automotive
13. Miscellaneous

Each of these general categories is further subdivided into numerical listings and subtitles. For example, the areas of Employment and Outdoor Sports look something like this:

| **Employment** | **Outdoor Sports** |
|---|---|
| 030 Accounting | 600 Campers |
| 031 Help Wanted | 601 Motor Homes |
| 032 Part-Time Help | 603 Bicycles |
| 033 Data Processing | 610 Boats and Motors |
| 035 Health Care | 620 Motorcycles |

## Searching the Want Ads

Jennifer has been searching for a used mountain bike. She knows she can save a great deal of money if she reads the classified ads.

How would she find mountain bikes in the newspaper? First, Jennifer would look for the Classified Section. This is listed in the *Index*. After turning to the *Classified Section*, she would then review the

*General Categories.* Since biking is a sport, she would look for *Outdoor Sports.* Under this heading is *603 Bicycles.* Mountain bikes for females would be specifically noted. There is generally a list of the abbreviations used at the beginning of the classifieds, where Jennifer could find difficult ones she could not guess.

In Nicholas's case, he would review the *General Categories* for *Employment* and then *032 Part-Time Help* to find job ads in his area. To find a used motorbike, he would look under *Outdoor Sports* for *620 Motorcycles.*

Maria's ad for a garage sale would be included under *Merchandise.* The title *482 Garage, House, Apt. Sales* would be listed here. People could easily find a list of upcoming garage sales in their area.

By scanning the classified section, it becomes easy to find whatever you may be looking for. Each newspaper has its own way of classifying and numbering ads, but it's easy to figure out, if you just look at it for a few minutes.

# EXAMPLES OF CLASSIFIED ADS

**A**fter buying the Sunday paper, Nicholas began his search for a part-time job and a motorbike. He found the Classified Section easily, then moved to the Employment title and finally to Part-Time Help, where jobs were listed alphabetically. Nicholas found two jobs that sounded interesting. Here is what he discovered:

---

032    Part-Time Help

---

DELIVERY PERSON. Deliver flyers for small local company in dwnt. area. Min.wage. Must present gd. appearance and be able to work two afternoons per week. Store 764 Main St. Apply in per. 3-5 P.M. on Wed. 4/24/94.

---

Highlight ads that interest you as you scan the classified section of the newspaper.

---

OFFICE ASSISTANT. PT office work for church. Hours—Mon.-Tues.-Wed. 3-6 P.M. Mature, dependable, some office equip. skills helpful. Call or send resume to First Lutheran Church, 132 Maple St., Kirkwood, Pa. 10222 tel: 555-5666.

---

The first job was delivering flyers—which meant he would be doing a lot of door-to-door work in the downtown area and, in all types of weather. It paid the minimum wage, which is now $4.50 per hour. The job demanded a neat and clean appearance. Two afternoons were required, but it did not say which ones. This would be a question to ask at the interview. The company was located downtown, which was quite a distance from Nicholas's home. Getting to work could be a problem since he did not have access to a car. It would take 30 minutes by bus. The ad stated he must apply in person on Wednesday afternoon. Nicholas would find out more about the job when he went to apply.

The second job was part-time office work. The days and times were listed. Nicholas did have some knowledge of business. He had typing skills which he had learned at school. He felt he was responsible and mature. One of the advantages of this job was that the church was very close to his school. The job required three days' work instead of two, which probably meant more money. Nicholas planned to call about the job and if it sounded interesting, he would send his resume.

Nicholas found only one motorbike under 620 Motorcycles, which was listed under Outdoor Sports.

---

620 Motorcycles

---

HONDA MOTORBIKE. '88 Low mileage. Gd. Condition. Must See. $1200/B.O. 555-1007 aft. 6 P.M.

---

This particular ad sounded good to Nicholas. The motorbike was in good condition and had low mileage. The list of abbreviations gave B.O. as "best offer." This meant that the bike would sell for $1200 or the best offer. The ad included a number to call after 6 P.M. However, Nicholas would need to raise the money before he could even consider buying a bike. Because he had very little money, his job search became more important.

## Jennifer's Search

Jennifer reviewed Outdoor Sports for ads relating to mountain bikes. Under 603 Bicycles, she found two ads that attracted her attention.

---

603 Bicycle

---

MTN BIKE Female model, 21 speed Navy/ Green. Extras. 20". Orig. $450. Asking $300 w/lock. 555-6692 betw. 7-9 P.M.

MOUNTAIN BIKE-18", 18 spd. Ex. Cond./ Ladies. Must sell. Extras Available. Used 2x. $200/ B.O. Call 555-6890 after 7 P.M.

Each of these ads offered Jennifer the opportunity to buy a mountain bike at a lower cost than a new one. The first bike had more speeds and extra options, possibly a speedometer or a basket. It was also more money. There was a number listed to call between 7 and 9 P.M.

The second bike had fewer speeds and was smaller in size. Extras were available, but it was not clear whether they were installed on the bike. She might have to pay for installation. The ad stated the bike was used only twice, which made it almost new. It was selling for $200, which was $100 less than the other bike. There may also have been some flexibility in the price since B.O. or best offer was listed. A phone number was provided to call after 7 P.M.

Calling about both of these bikes, asking questions, and looking at them would help Jennifer decide. She could make a more informed decision about which one might be the better deal.

Classified ads try to communicate in the briefest and clearest manner. Checking them frequently helps readers become familiar with the way the ads are organized, how they are written, and how words are abbreviated.

—

**Before you shop, decide on the amount you want to spend.**

# THE LANGUAGE OF THE CLASSIFIEDS

**W**hen people place ads in newspapers or magazines, they want to attract the attention of the public. They wish to increase their chances of hiring, buying, selling or trading by reaching as many people as possible.

In order to do this, they must present information that is clear, concise and understandable. These ads are usually short since there is a per line charge. The goal is to put the greatest amount of information in the shortest amount of space. Normally, this can be done in three lines or less. Businesses or corporations can spend more.

There is a great deal of simplified terminology or wording that is unique to the classifieds. Advertisers often use initials and abbreviations to simplify their ads and cut costs. New readers of classified

---

**Reading through classified advertising may give you an idea for creating an ad of your own.**

ads may have some difficulty understanding what these shortened terms mean.

It takes some time and patience to learn what these ads mean since not all of the abbreviations are listed at the beginning of the want ads. By reading the classifieds regularly, you will find it easier to interpret the language they are using.

You can make up your own abbreviations, just by playing with the letters and sounds. Don't be afraid to experiment, there are no fixed rules, the whole idea is to make yourself understood. Be creative, ask friends and relatives to read your abbreviations to see that others understand them—have fun with it.

To help begin this process, here is a list of initials and abbreviations:

1. *K* = $1000 (example — 5K = $5,000)
2. *E.O.E.* = Equal Opportunity Employer Complies with federal and state laws against discrimination on the basis of race, creed, color, or disabilities.
3. *$5/hr* = $5.00 per hour
4. 75 *wpm* typing = typing 75 words per minute
5. *Job Info* = Job Information
6. *Attn.* Joe Smith = for the attention of Joe Smith
7. *1/800*-555-9570 = You do not pay long distance charges when calling an 800 number. You are charged for a local call, and the other party pays the additional charges.
8. *C/O* = in care of
9. *Min.* = Minimum; *Max.* = Maximum

10. *Mos.* = Months; *Yrs.* = Years

11. *Job List Svc. Fee $100* = Job List Service Fee = $100. You must pay the $100 fee if you accept and are placed in the job. This is an ad placed by an employment agency.

12. 555-9200 *ext.* 262 = extension 262—ask for it when you call.

13. *Exp.* = Experience

14. *Ex. Cond.* = Excellent Condition

15. *Apply In Person* = Go to the address listed, without calling or writing first.

16. *Car Req'd.* = Car is required, and it is supplied by you.

17. *M/F* = Male/Female

18. *Circa* 1890s = Around the 1890s

19. *FT* = Full-Time; *PT* = Part-Time

20. *Int'l* = International

21. *Pref.* = Preferred

22. *Aft.* = After

23. *B.O.* = Best Offer

24. *Betw.* = Between

25. *W/Lock* = With Lock

26. *x* = By: Example; 2'x 4'; or 2 feet by 4 feet.

    *x* = Times: Example; 2x per week; or 2 times per week.

# CHAPTER 4

# FOLLOWING UP ON CLASSIFIEDS

**T**here are three ways to answer classified ads. The first is by phone. Many ads will list a phone number to call. Pay particular attention to what time to call. Usually a specific time will be given such as "between 7-9 P.M." or "after 5 P.M." Both the ads for mountain bikes gave specific times to call.

Although one of the ads Nicholas was interested in gave a phone number, it did not specify a particular time to call. Some time during the business day (9-5) would be the right time to call.

When you answer an ad by phone, be polite and use appropriate phone manners. Ask for more information about the job or merchandise. This gives the one who is advertising an opportunity to

---

**Your interview will be more productive if you take some time beforehand to prepare yourself.**

describe the job or item in detail. Before phoning, jot down specific questions you wish to ask. This helps you organize your thoughts. Make sure you ask the price of the merchandise over the phone.

When you are looking for a job, you can discuss the salary or hourly wage at the interview, *not* over the phone.

If the phone conversation is positive, then schedule an appointment to examine the merchandise or to set up an interview.

The second way to answer a classified ad is to go in person. One of the ads Nicholas was interested in, asked for this. Nicholas will be judged on his appearance, as well as how he handles himself at the interview.

When you go to an interview, be prepared to discuss duties, responsibilities, and salary. Write questions on notecards to refresh your memory. Be neat, clean, enthusiastic, and ready to talk about yourself.

The third way to answer a classified ad is by mail. The ad will normally list an address or box number. In this instance, send a typed resume and a cover letter. The resume summarizes your skills and experience. The cover letter expresses your interest and enthusiasm for the job. Your goal is to attract positive attention and obtain a job interview.

The mail provides employers with an opportunity to screen prospective candidates. If they are impressed with your credentials, they will call you for an interview. If not, they might send you a form letter thanking you for applying, but declining your application. Not everyone responds to you.

As you begin to make contacts, there is one thing to remember—everything is negotiable. For instance, a seller usually asks more than he/she expects. Once you examine the merchandise, offer a sum that you feel is fair and reasonable, but below the asking price. The seller may make a counter-offer below the asking price, but higher than what you offered. At this point you can decide to take the offer, or think about it for a day or so. Use the time to consider if the merchandise is worth the price. You may have second thoughts. Patience is always important in trying to make a deal. How-ever, another buyer could be in the wings, willing to pay the asking price. This is the chance you take. It all depends on how much you want to pay and how badly you need the merchandise.

Once you have negotiated a salary or bought and sold items, the process becomes easier for you. You will become more confident and accustomed to the marketplace. It is important to remember that sometimes you win, and sometimes you lose.

Be prepared to experience both winning and losing. Over time, you will strengthen your negoti-ating skills.

Develop a win-win attitude, and you will be happy with the results. Win-win means that both parties involved in the transaction feel satisfied that a fair deal has been made, that everybody won, and nobody lost.

Don't be afraid to question the price of an item. There may be a saving in buying large quantities, or a price reduction on an item that is slightly damaged.

# LEARNING HOW TO
# PLACE AN AD

**M**aria decided the best
way to advertise her garage sale was in the local
newspaper. But since she had never placed an ad
before, she was uncertain about how to do it.
Maria got a copy of the paper and checked the
classified section. Here she found the information
she needed about rates and deadlines.

Much of this information was a bit confusing. So
she called the classified department at the paper.
Maria spoke with Mrs. Thompson and explained
she needed to place an ad for her garage sale.

The classified department offered different ad
rates for businesses and private individuals or families. Businesses were charged by the number of

Whether you are creating an ad or answering one, make sure
your work is neat, and your message is clear and brief.

lines and how often the ads would run. Private
individuals and families were charged lower rates.
These particular rates offered three lines for four or
seven consecutive days in the paper.

Mrs. Thompson suggested to Maria that she take
advantage of the lower rate that offered three lines
for the four consecutive days before the sale. This
would cost her $28.50. Seven days would have cost
$37.50. Mrs. Thompson explained that most ga-
rage-sale hunters checked the papers for sales taking
place in the next three to four days. Since Maria's
garage sale would be on Saturday of the following
week, her ad should run Tuesday through Friday.

Maria would have to place the ad with the classified department by Monday at 6 P.M. It would also
have to be paid for at that time.

Deadlines for placing specific ads were listed in
the classified section. Mrs. Thompson emphasized
how important it was to plan ahead and meet the
time limits.

## Creating an Ad

Maria then began to work on what her ad would
say. She realized it would be difficult to limit the
information to her three line minimum. Her ad
needed to attract positive attention. It also needed
to communicate several things. First, it had to state
what she was offering. Maria would have to be very
selective here. Next, it had to state her address,
phone number, date, and time of the garage sale.

After a great deal of writing and revising, Maria created the following ad:

---

### 482 Garage Sales

---

BETHEL PARK – 214 Maple Rd. Oakhurst Section. April 5, 8 A.M. – 5 P.M. Furn., clothes, glassware, rugs, records, baseball cards, etc. 958-2500.

---

She included all the basic information, and limited the items to those things that people want the most. Notice this was all she could squeeze into the three lines she was given. Maria was happy that this ad would run for the four consecutive days before the sale. She was hoping for a big crowd.

## Deadlines

Deadlines are the times when ads need to be placed, for publication. Newspapers follow these rules strictly so that there is enough time for typesetting. Check with the newspaper to find out the individual deadlines for each category of classified ads. The deadlines vary.

Maria remembered that Mrs. Thompson said the deadline for placing the ad would be Monday at 6 P.M. She could have called the ad in, but decided to write it out and hand-deliver it to make sure it was on time and just right.

# Payment for the Ad

There are several ways that classified ads can be paid for. They can be paid for by cash, check, or credit card. Immediately upon payment by cash or credit card, work on the ad can begin. But one must allow an extra day or two for a check to clear; only then will the work start. When the ad is paid in full, it will be run in the newspaper. This is the usual business practice.

Maria decided to pay in cash when she placed the ad to make sure it would make the Monday evening deadline.

You should be given a receipt for your ad. If you do not get one, as you pay, then ask for the receipt. You may not feel that you need it, but there are several reasons why you do.

One reason is, this is the right place to practice good business and life skills. When people are rushing you, you have to speak up politely and explain that you need a receipt for your records.

Another reason for keeping a receipt, is that businesses often make mistakes, and the record of your payment can get lost. If this happens, you might be asked to pay again, because you can't produce proof of payment.

# USING CLASSIFIEDS WISELY

**T**here are many advantages to using the classified ads. Since people are always on the lookout for bargains, there is a feeling of personal satisfaction when they feel they have shopped wisely.

Newspaper classifieds provide a great deal of information about jobs and merchandise. They are a low cost, convenient way to advertise.

Ads provide immediate leads. New information is published every day. It can be advantageous to read these ads daily. Sunday is the big classified day, so this day is a must for reading.

The classifieds save time and can reach many people in the community. Prices are reasonable and within most people's budgets. The way newspapers and magazines present their ads is well-organized and easy to read.

However, the classifieds should be used in conjunction with other advertising methods, such as networking.

Networking means telling as many people as possible that you are looking for a job or for specific merchandise.

Following up on help wanted signs, and door-to-door soliciting are other ways that can be useful. Every method requires patience and perseverance.

## Using Caution

When you use the classifieds, always be cautious. There are many unscrupulous and unethical people in the world who try to take advantage of unsuspecting readers. They often target young people, whose inexperience makes them vulnerable.

Their main goal is to rip you off and take your money without any risk to themselves. Be cautious in your approach and examine each situation. Seek adult advice if you have questions or feel uncertain about a particular situation. In the business world, *"Let the Buyer Beware"* applies. Keep a positive attitude, but be careful.

The same warning applies to employment ads. There are some employers who like to take advantage of prospective employees. They want you to work for almost nothing and they seek to monopolize your time. Analyze these situations carefully

—

**Check all purchases (new or used) carefully.**

and never sign anything without adult advice. Do
not rush. Do not enter into anything if an inter-
viewer puts pressure on you. Proceed slowly and
cautiously. There are always other opportunities
right around the corner.

Your main goal is to try to make a deal where
both parties are happy and satisfied. Think about
this when you read the classified ads.

## Summary

By using the classified ads, Nicholas, Jennifer, and
Maria succeeded in finding what each of them
wanted. They kept their minds open, and enjoyed
the adventure and new experiences. They were
careful to remember the warnings and cautions.
They did not jump at the first things that presented
themselves.

They were also very clear in their own minds
exactly what they wanted and needed. They con-
sulted with young friends and also with older
people, so they could learn from other people's
experiences.

## Nicholas

Nicholas's search for a part-time job and a used
motorbike required hard work. Although he
applied for the two jobs listed in the paper, he was
not successful in landing either one. However, he
was not discouraged. Nicholas remained positive in

his attitude and continued to check the classifieds every day. A part-time job at an ice cream parlor appeared in the classified section several days later. This job was only three blocks from his home. He was interviewed and got the job. Nicholas was extremely happy.

His search for the motorbike would have to wait. Most of the bikes he found were too expensive. He realized he would have to begin saving his money. Nicholas now had a goal to work toward.

# Jennifer

Jennifer's dream of owning a mountain bike became a reality. She was able to make a deal with the woman who was selling the 18-speed ladies' mountain bike. It had only been used twice and the asking price was $200. After inspecting the bike, Jennifer was able to negotiate the price down to $175. She felt very proud of herself for getting an almost new bike at such a low cost. That left her money to buy the extras for her bike.

# Maria

Maria used the classifieds to advertise her garage sale. While her ad was running (for the four consecutive days prior to the sale), she had numerous calls. The response was varied, and some people asked for directions to her house, while others simply inquired about the merchandise.

Maria's garage sale was a huge success. She was able to raise enough money to make her dream of owning the convertible come true. There was even enough money left over to buy some clothes.

Both Maria and her parents were proud of her efforts in organizing and planning the garage sale.

The experiences that Nicholas, Jennifer, and Maria had, demonstrate that the classified ads can be a valuable resource.

There is one caution to follow. Use only phone numbers in your ads. For safety, do not give your name and address to callers until you verify their phone numbers. Ask for the caller's name, address, and telephone number, and say you'll call back. Check the phone book, or call information; the name must match the address, and the phone number must be the same. Don't call back if any of these do not match.

It is good to remember there are always many ways to earn money—you will always find different opportunities, and a lot of these you can make for yourself.

Try placing an ad in the Services Offered category. You can offer things like the following:

- Student will shop for you, (clothing, food, gifts…).
- Light typing or word processing available.
- Bilingual student will write letters for you.
- Student seeks after school work.
- Student seeks apprenticeship in ad agency, (publishing, retailing, car repairing).

To make your own opportunities, look for other people's needs. Search for them. What can I do? Where can I search? When you run out of ideas, you can search for advice, and this will start up your energy and your ideas again.

How do I find out about...? Practice asking other people this question, practice not feeling funny or embarrassed, it is a skill that you can use all your life.

You can look for a summer job helping to re-model or redecorate a house, perhaps working for a contractor. If you have the ability to search and succeed, you will be useful. You can help find materials wanted at the last minute, or help locate delayed shipments; and the skills you develop in buying cars or bikes will be useful in buying build-ing materials or paint.

Skills are always transferable. You use the things you know to solve the problems you don't know. Good luck! Search and succeed.

# GLOSSARY
## EXPLAINING NEW WORDS

**ads** Short word for advertising or advertisements.

**bargain** To negotiate an agreeable exchange. (Not related to bargain price.)

**bargain price** An unusually low price.

**barter** To trade one thing for another, by direct exchange. Money is not involved.

**buyer** One who receives something in exchange for payment.

**classified ads** Ads arranged by subject matter (class or category).

**classified rates** Price of placing an ad in the classifieds.

**classified section** The section of a newspaper or magazine where classified ads appear.

**contact** As a verb; to get in touch with someone. As a noun; a person you are in touch with. For example, "She is my contact in that office."

**convenient** Easy to use, easy to do, easy to reach.

**cover letter** A letter that accompanies a resume. It introduces you, and explains anything you wish to communicate.

**credentials** 1. In education, official certification of the completion of a course of study. 2. Letters of commendation, that provide a basis for confidence in you. 3. Accomplishments that you can describe, to show your worth in business.

**deadline** The cut-off time for a payment, or application, or submission of documents.

**goods and services** Goods are things. Goods and services are things which people offer for sale.

**green sheets** A newspaper which is distributed free, containing local consumer advertising. It is often on green paper.

**index** An alphabetical list of what's in a book or newspaper. Most publications have an index.

**in person** To appear physically, not by letter, or phone.

**negotiate** To talk with someone in order to reach an agreement.

**networking** Communicating with people in order to exchange information. This is a good way to look for a job.

**perseverance** Persistence in reaching a goal. Staying with it, in spite of difficulties.

**prospective** Expected with confidence.

**resource** Something or someone that can aid or support you.

**resume** A history of one's qualifications and experience.

**seller** One who receives money in exchange for goods or services.

**solicit** To ask for something. To approach someone with a request.

**solicitor** A person who asks you to buy something.

**unscrupulous** Having no principles. Someone who takes advantage of others.

**want ads** Another name for classified ads.

# FOR FURTHER READING

Carey, Helen H., and Greenberg, Judith E. *How to Read a Newspaper.* New York: Franklin Watts, 1983.

McFarland, Rhoda. *The World of Work.* New York: Rosen Publishing Group, 1993.

Milios, Rita. *Shopping Savvy.* New York: Rosen Publishing Group, 1993.

Reynolds, Moira. *The Telephone: Uses and Abuses.* New York: Rosen Publishing Group, 1993.

Santamaria, Peggy. *Money Smarts.* New York: Rosen Publishing Group, 1993.

# INDEX

## About the Author

Bruce McGlothlin is a school psychologist/counselor in the Alleghany Intermediate Unit in Pittsburgh, Pennsylvania. He holds graduate degrees in both school psychology and counseling. He is the author of *Traveling Light*, a guide to self-exploration for adolescents, and *Great Grooming for Guys*, a book offering practical advice on personal cleanliness, health, diet, exercise, and clothes.

Bruce and his wife, Judi, are the parents of two teenagers, Michael and Molly. Bruce's hobbies include: ultra-marathon running, biking, reading, and doing jigsaw puzzles.

## Photo Credits

All photos on cover and in book by Mary Lauzon.

**Design & Production by Blackbirch Graphics, Inc.**